A DAY IN THE LIFE OF A
Circus Clown

by Carol Gaskin
Photography by John F. Klein

Troll Associates

Library of Congress Cataloging in Publication Data

Gaskin, Carol.
   A day in the life of a circus clown.

   Summary: Follows a circus clown through his day as
he practices routines, cares for costumes and props,
applies make-up, and entertains the audience.
    1. Clowns—Juvenile literature. [1. Clowns
2. Gosh, Omar. 3. Circus. 4. Occupations] I. Klein,
John F. (John Frederick), 1950-   ill. II. Title.
GV1828.G37   1988   791.3'3   87-10954
ISBN 0-8167-1107-0 (lib. bdg.)
ISBN 0-8167-1108-9 (pbk.)

The author and publisher wish to thank the staff of Allan C. Hill Entertainment Corp., especially Allan C. Hill, Fred John, and Jeffrey Scott; Mike Ridenour, Jim Ridenour, and the performers and staff of Great American Circus.
Special thanks to Charles Neubauer of Sarasota, Florida. Photograph on page
5 by Fred John, courtesy of Allan C. Hill Entertainment Corp.

Mike Ridenour is a clown in a traveling circus.
Every morning he wakes up in a new town. During the night, the circus travels in a caravan, or
long line of trucks and trailers. The trucks arrive
at an empty field at dawn. By midday, the circus
will spring to life once again.

As the sun rises, workers called "roustabouts" raise the Big Top. The tent will cover two-thirds the area of a football field. First, tent stakes are driven into the ground and tent poles are laid out. Then the tent is unrolled from a special truck, called a "spool wagon."

The roustabouts spread the canvas over the metal poles that will support the roof. They anchor the sides of the tent to the wooden tent stakes. Later, when the heavy tent poles are raised, the tent will go up with them. To do this, very special equipment will be needed—elephants!

The elephants are harnessed to the poles. They pull, and up goes the tent! Circus tents have been raised this way for generations. When it rains, elephants are also used to pull trucks and trailers out of the mud. So many circus vehicles get stuck that traveling circuses are often called "mud-shows."

Mike has free time while the tent goes up. He practices an acrobatic routine with Chepi, a seven-year-old clown. Most clowns learn their trade from older clowns. Mike's first teacher was his father. Now Chepi, whose parents are bareback riders in the circus, learns clowning from Mike. It's a circus tradition.

Mike washes in cold water from a huge water truck. He naps in the shade of another truck. Circus life is not always comfortable! The circus is like a town on wheels. The performers ride, wash, eat and sleep in the eighteen-wheelers that have replaced the circus wagons of the old days.

Being a clown is not all clowning. Mike must care for his costumes and props. He grooms his clown wig and practices on a miniature trumpet he sometimes uses in his act. Some days he works on his juggling or stilt-walking. His act is always changing as he masters new skills.

An hour before showtime, Mike applies his make-up, or "puts on his face." First he coats his face with white grease paint. He smiles and frowns to study the creases and hollows his facial muscles make. Then he outlines spaces where he will wipe the white grease paint away.

Mike fills in the spaces with flesh color. There are several classic clown types: the neat whiteface, the unshaven tramp, and the colorful Auguste. Mike is an Auguste-type clown. An Auguste clown has a flesh-toned face and wears bright, baggy clothes. The jokes are always played on him.

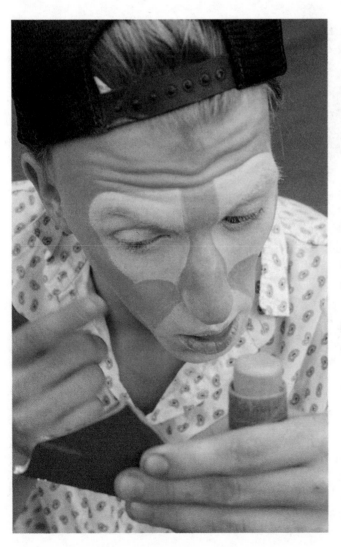
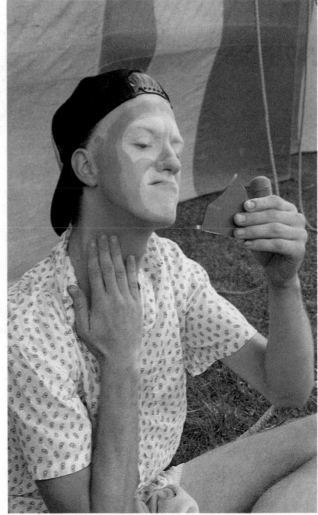

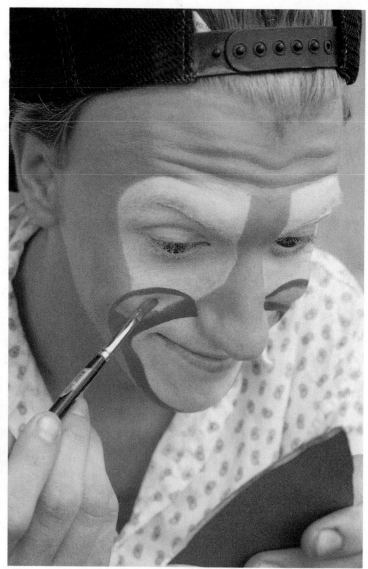

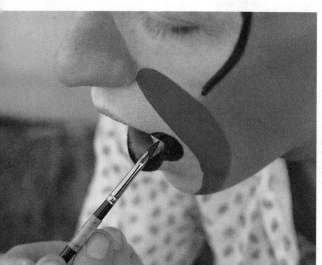

A clown's face is as personal as his signature. Mike adds the detailing that makes his face his own. He paints his cheeks cherry red and adds touches of black to his eyes and mouth. Soon he will assume his clown personality, a goofy character named Omar Gosh.

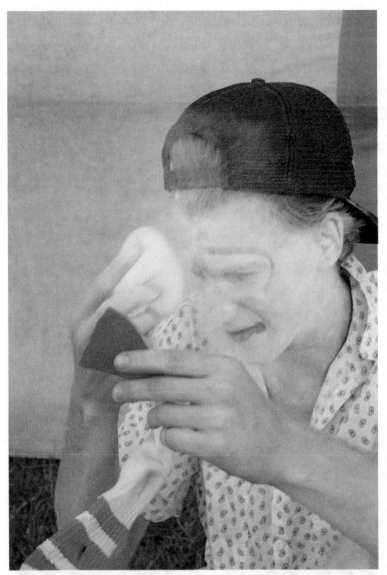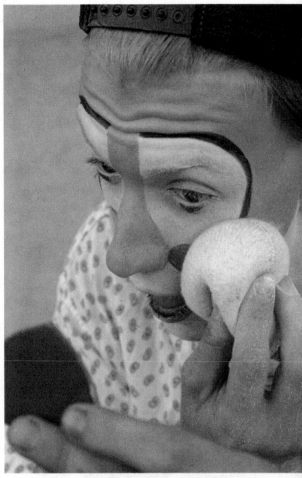

Mike fills an old sock with baby powder and powders his face. "Don't you wonder what happens to all of those socks you lose?" he asks. "They travel all over the world. Clowns have them!" Finally, to "fix" his face, Mike blots the excess powder for a smooth finish.

Mike dresses in the costume he has picked for the day. He always wears baggy pants, suspenders, and a loud shirt. He finds some of his costumes in second-hand stores. His giant-sized clown shoes come from a mail-order company. Mike wears out two pairs every season.

As Mike adds the finishing touches, he says, "When most kids think of a clown, they think of great big shoes and a red nose." Omar Gosh always has both. He puts on a bright false nose, a silly little hat, a big smile, and *Presto!* Say "hello" to Omar Gosh!

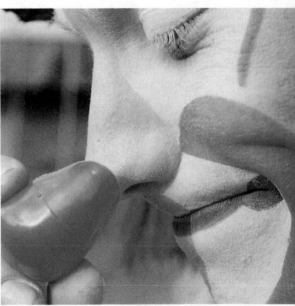

It's showtime! The audience streams toward the entrance to the Big Top. They must walk along the "midway"—a broad avenue lined with rides and concession stands. The air smells of circus animals, peanuts, and cotton candy. Inside the Big Top, the music starts, and people buzz with excitement.

The ringmaster blows his whistle and introduces the first act. "Ladies and Gentlemen, Boys and Girls," he announces. "Presenting—that juggling genius, Jose Torres!" It's the ringmaster's job to make sure each act is ready on time, and to see that the show flows smoothly.

Animal acts are the heart of the circus, and animal trainers are highly respected. The audience *oohs* and *aahs* as acrobats ride trick ponies, elephants dance, and fearless trainers work with ferocious jungle cats. But if animals are the heart of the circus, clowns are its soul.

The clowns do an old routine called "Queen Bee." "Hey, Coco," says Omar Gosh, "give me something sweet!" Coco replies, "How about some honey?" Omar exclaims, "Oh, I love honey!" Then Coco buzzes around the ring, saying, "I'm the worker bee, collecting honey for the queen bee!"

Coco says, "When you say 'Let it fly!' I'll give you the honey." But when Omar isn't looking, Coco secretly fills his mouth with water. Omar says, "Yum, honey! Let it fly!" The crowd explodes with laughter as the "honey" splashes in Omar's face!

Omar decides to play the same trick on Little
Dave. "I'll be the worker bee," he says. But he
trips and loses his "honey." While Omar gets a re-
fill, Little Dave sneaks a mouthful too. When
Little Dave doesn't say anything, Omar swallows
his "honey" and cries, "You're supposed to say,
'Let it fly!'"

Little Dave "lets it fly" and Omar Gosh gets showered again. The crowd roars. Omar is used to being the one who always "gets it." It's his traditional role. "Making people laugh is what being a clown is all about," he says. And he always gets a laugh.

After changing into a dry costume, Omar sells coloring books in the stands. It is an important part of his job with the circus because it allows him to get closer to the audience. He can joke with the children, shake their hands, and autograph their souvenir books.

Between shows, Omar works on the midway. To help advertise the circus, he gives an interview to a disc jockey from a local radio station. Then he greets the children on the train ride, who are thrilled to meet a real clown. Promoting good public relations is a serious responsibility for a circus clown.

While some acts are performing under the Big Top, others are getting ready behind the scenes. The elephant trainer rehearses with his elephants, and a bareback rider climbs into a furry gorilla suit. They must be ready to enter the ring when the ringmaster announces their acts.

Omar stops to talk with the other clowns on the midway. As a youngster passes, Coco holds out his hand and says, "Give me five!" The excited boy slaps Coco's hand with glee, then hurries down the midway. The last show is about to begin, so Omar heads for the Big Top.

The clowns run into the center ring. Little Dave announces, "Tonight I will perform my world famous egg-juggling routine. When I count to three, I'm going to throw this egg into the air and catch it in my back pocket! One . . . two . . ." Omar looks up, then runs. But Little Dave doesn't throw the egg.

"*Everyone* has to count!" insists Little Dave. "One . . . two . . . wait a minute! That lady *still* isn't counting!" Again and again he delays. Finally, the whole audience yells, "THREE!" and Little Dave throws the egg into the air. The crowd screams with delight as the egg lands right on Little Dave's head!

As Mike and the other clowns get ready for the grand finale, Chepi helps out with a routine everyone loves. The circus ring has become a boxing ring, and the star performer is a boxing kangaroo! Chepi rings a bell to signal the end of each round.

At night the midway is a magical place. It seems to glow with a light of its own. Children are up past their bedtimes. Full of popcorn and cotton candy, they clutch their souvenir balloons. Tonight they will dream of bareback riders, dancing elephants, and smiling clowns.

Behind the scenes, Omar Gosh and Coco share a quiet moment before the finale. Even though the show is almost over, circus clowns must always be ready to perform. If there is an accident in the Big Top or if someone is late, the ringmaster will "send in the clowns."

Omar leads the circus finale. The performers march around the ring waving flags. A giant flag unfurls behind the clowns, and the circus comes to a close. Tonight, Omar Gosh will remove his makeup and fall asleep. Tomorrow, Mike Ridenour will wake up in a new town—and the circus tent will rise again.